EMMANUEL JOSEPH

Virtuous Ventures, Building a Life of Faith, Ethics, and Career Fulfillment

Copyright © 2025 by Emmanuel Joseph

All rights reserved. No part of this publication may be reproduced, stored or transmitted in any form or by any means, electronic, mechanical, photocopying, recording, scanning, or otherwise without written permission from the publisher. It is illegal to copy this book, post it to a website, or distribute it by any other means without permission.

First edition

This book was professionally typeset on Reedsy. Find out more at reedsy.com

Contents

1	Chapter 1	1
2	Chapter 1: Foundations of Faith and Ethics	4
3	Chapter 2: Discovering Your Life's Purpose	6
4	Chapter 3: Balancing Faith and Career Ambitions	8
5	Chapter 4: Ethical Decision-Making in the Workplace	10
6	Chapter 5: Building Authentic Relationships	12
7	Chapter 6: Embracing Life's Challenges with Grace	14
8	Chapter 7: Cultivating a Strong Work Ethic	16
9	Chapter 8: Nurturing a Spirit of Gratitude	18
10	Chapter 9: The Power of Compassion and Kindness	20
11	Chapter 10: Leading with Integrity	22
12	Chapter 11: Pursuing Lifelong Learning	24
13	Chapter 12: Leaving a Lasting Legacy	26

1

Chapter 1

Introduction: Virtuous Ventures: Building a Life of Faith, Ethics, and Career Fulfillment

In an ever-evolving world where rapid advancements in technology, shifting cultural norms, and complex global challenges shape our daily lives, the quest for a meaningful and purpose-driven existence remains a timeless pursuit. "Virtuous Ventures: Building a Life of Faith, Ethics, and Career Fulfillment" delves into this profound journey, exploring the interplay between faith, ethics, and career aspirations. This book is designed to guide readers toward a holistic approach to personal and professional growth, emphasizing the importance of aligning one's actions with deeply held values and beliefs.

Faith and ethics serve as the foundation upon which a virtuous life is built. While faith provides a sense of purpose and a connection to something greater than ourselves, ethics govern our actions and interactions, ensuring that we navigate the complexities of life with integrity and compassion. The synergy between faith and ethics fosters a sense of authenticity and fulfillment, empowering individuals to lead lives that are both meaningful and impactful. This book aims to illuminate the paths toward integrating these principles into every facet of our existence.

Career fulfillment, often pursued in isolation from personal values, can lead to a sense of disconnection and dissatisfaction. However, when career aspirations are harmonized with faith and ethical principles, they become powerful avenues for personal growth and societal contribution. By aligning professional endeavors with core values, individuals can achieve not only material success but also a profound sense of purpose and satisfaction. This book offers insights and strategies for achieving this delicate balance, empowering readers to pursue careers that resonate with their deepest convictions.

Throughout history, individuals who have successfully integrated faith and ethics into their careers have made remarkable contributions to society. From visionary leaders to everyday heroes, their stories serve as powerful reminders of the transformative potential of virtuous living. This book draws inspiration from these exemplary lives, providing readers with practical guidance and timeless wisdom to navigate their own journeys. By exploring the principles and practices that have guided these individuals, readers can uncover their own paths to virtuous ventures.

In addition to historical examples, this book offers contemporary perspectives on the challenges and opportunities of integrating faith and ethics into modern careers. The fast-paced and often competitive nature of today's professional landscape can make it difficult to stay true to one's values. This book addresses these challenges head-on, providing readers with the tools and strategies needed to navigate ethical dilemmas, maintain authenticity, and cultivate a sense of purpose in their careers. By embracing these principles, individuals can thrive in their professional lives while staying grounded in their faith and values.

Moreover, "Virtuous Ventures" emphasizes the importance of community and collaboration in the pursuit of a virtuous life. Building a network of like-minded individuals who share similar values and aspirations can provide invaluable support and encouragement. This book explores the significance of authentic relationships and the power of collective action in fostering positive change. By cultivating a sense of community and collaboration, individuals can amplify their impact and contribute to a more just and compassionate world.

Ultimately, "Virtuous Ventures: Building a Life of Faith, Ethics, and Career

CHAPTER 1

Fulfillment" is a call to action for individuals seeking to lead lives of purpose and integrity. It invites readers to embark on a journey of self-discovery and growth, guided by the principles of faith and ethics. By integrating these values into their personal and professional lives, readers can achieve a harmonious balance that fosters fulfillment, resilience, and lasting impact. This book serves as a comprehensive guide to navigating the complexities of modern life with grace and purpose, empowering individuals to embark on their own virtuous ventures.

2

Chapter 1: Foundations of Faith and Ethics

Faith and ethics form the bedrock of a virtuous life. While faith provides a sense of purpose and understanding beyond the physical world, ethics governs our daily actions and interactions. Together, they guide individuals towards a fulfilling and morally sound existence. A life anchored in faith and ethics is not only spiritually rewarding but also fosters trust and respect within communities. The harmony between faith and ethics shapes our character and influences our decisions, ultimately leading to a more cohesive and compassionate society.

Throughout history, faith has played a pivotal role in shaping civilizations. From ancient rituals to modern-day worship, faith offers a lens through which people view the world and their place within it. It transcends cultural and geographical boundaries, uniting diverse groups under shared beliefs. This collective faith nurtures a sense of belonging and purpose, encouraging individuals to strive for a higher moral standard. The interwoven nature of faith and ethics ensures that our spiritual and moral compass remains aligned, guiding us towards virtuous ventures.

Ethics, on the other hand, is the practical manifestation of our moral values. It governs our actions, decisions, and interactions, ensuring that we act with integrity and respect. Ethical principles are deeply ingrained in our daily lives, influencing everything from personal relationships to professional conduct. By adhering to ethical standards, we create a foundation of trust and accountability, which is essential for building strong, lasting connections. The symbiotic relationship between faith and ethics fosters a holistic approach to personal growth and fulfillment.

In a world where material success often overshadows moral values, it is crucial to recognize the importance of faith and ethics in achieving true fulfillment. By cultivating a strong foundation in these principles, individuals can navigate life's challenges with grace and resilience. This holistic approach not only enhances personal well-being but also contributes to the greater good, creating a ripple effect of positive change. Embracing faith and ethics as guiding principles empowers individuals to lead virtuous ventures, paving the way for a more just and compassionate world.

3

Chapter 2: Discovering Your Life's Purpose

Discovering one's life purpose is a deeply personal and transformative journey. It involves introspection, exploration, and a willingness to embrace change. A clear sense of purpose provides direction and motivation, guiding individuals towards meaningful and fulfilling endeavors. This journey often begins with a process of self-reflection, where individuals examine their values, passions, and strengths. By understanding what truly matters to them, they can align their actions with their core beliefs, creating a life that is both purposeful and authentic.

The quest for purpose is not a linear path; it is often marked by twists and turns, setbacks, and breakthroughs. Embracing this uncertainty is essential, as it allows individuals to remain open to new possibilities and experiences. Along the way, they may encounter mentors, inspirations, and opportunities that help shape their understanding of their purpose. By remaining curious and adaptable, individuals can navigate the complexities of this journey with confidence and resilience, ultimately uncovering a purpose that resonates deeply with their true selves.

Purpose-driven living extends beyond personal fulfillment; it has a profound impact on the broader community. When individuals are aligned with their purpose, they are more likely to contribute positively to society, using their unique talents and passions to make a difference. This sense of contribution fosters a greater sense of connection and belonging, reinforcing the importance of purpose in creating a harmonious and thriving community. By pursuing their purpose with integrity and dedication, individuals can inspire others to embark on their own journeys, creating a collective movement towards positive change.

Ultimately, discovering one's life purpose is a continuous process of growth and evolution. As individuals progress on their journey, they may find that their purpose shifts and expands, reflecting their changing perspectives and experiences. Embracing this fluidity allows for a deeper understanding of oneself and a more profound connection to the world around them. By remaining committed to their values and passions, individuals can navigate the ever-changing landscape of life with grace and purpose, leading a life that is both fulfilling and impactful.

4

Chapter 3: Balancing Faith and Career Ambitions

Balancing faith and career ambitions can be challenging, but it is essential for achieving holistic fulfillment. Faith provides a moral framework that guides individuals in their professional lives, ensuring that their actions align with their core values. This alignment fosters a sense of integrity and authenticity, which is crucial for long-term success and satisfaction. By integrating faith into their career pursuits, individuals can create a harmonious balance between their spiritual and professional aspirations, leading to a more meaningful and purpose-driven life.

In the modern workplace, where competition and ambition often dominate, it is easy to lose sight of one's ethical principles. However, staying true to one's faith and values is essential for maintaining a sense of purpose and integrity. By prioritizing ethical conduct and compassion in their professional endeavors, individuals can build a reputation of trust and respect. This not only enhances their personal well-being but also contributes to a positive work environment, fostering collaboration and mutual support. The integration of faith and career ambitions creates a foundation of integrity that benefits both the individual and their community.

Moreover, balancing faith and career ambitions involves recognizing the importance of rest and reflection. In a fast-paced world, it is easy to become

CHAPTER 3: BALANCING FAITH AND CAREER AMBITIONS

consumed by professional demands, leading to burnout and disconnection from one's spiritual practice. By prioritizing regular moments of rest and introspection, individuals can maintain a healthy balance between their career and faith. This practice of self-care and reflection allows for a deeper connection to one's values and purpose, fostering resilience and clarity in the face of challenges. By nurturing both their spiritual and professional lives, individuals can achieve a more fulfilling and balanced existence.

Ultimately, the integration of faith and career ambitions is a dynamic and ongoing process. It requires continuous self-reflection, adaptability, and a commitment to one's core values. By embracing this holistic approach, individuals can navigate the complexities of modern life with grace and purpose, creating a career that is not only successful but also deeply aligned with their spiritual beliefs. This balance fosters a sense of fulfillment and authenticity, empowering individuals to lead virtuous ventures in both their personal and professional lives.

5

Chapter 4: Ethical Decision-Making in the Workplace

Ethical decision-making in the workplace is a critical aspect of professional integrity and success. It involves evaluating actions and choices through the lens of moral values, ensuring that decisions align with ethical principles. This process requires a deep understanding of one's core beliefs and a commitment to acting with integrity, even in the face of challenges or pressures. By prioritizing ethical decision-making, individuals can build a reputation of trust and respect, creating a positive and supportive work environment.

One of the key components of ethical decision-making is transparency. Clear and open communication is essential for fostering trust and accountability within the workplace. By being transparent about their intentions and actions, individuals can create a culture of honesty and integrity. This transparency extends to addressing potential conflicts of interest, seeking guidance from mentors, and collaborating with colleagues to ensure that decisions are made in the best interest of all stakeholders. Ethical decision-making requires a collective effort, where everyone is committed to upholding moral values and principles.

Another important aspect of ethical decision-making is empathy. Understanding the perspectives and experiences of others is crucial for making informed and compassionate choices. By considering the impact of their decisions on colleagues, clients, and the broader community, individuals can act with empathy and fairness. This empathetic approach fosters a supportive and inclusive work environment, where everyone feels valued and respected. By prioritizing empathy in their decision-making process, individuals can create a workplace that is not only ethical but also deeply connected to the well-being of all its members.

Ultimately, ethical decision-making in the workplace is an ongoing commitment to integrity and moral principles. It requires continuous self-reflection, a willingness to seek guidance, and the courage to act with honesty and compassion. By embracing this approach, individuals can navigate the complexities of professional life with confidence and purpose, creating a career that is both successful and ethically sound. This commitment to ethical decision-making empowers individuals to lead virtuous ventures in their professional lives, contributing to a more just and compassionate world.

6

Chapter 5: Building Authentic Relationships

Building authentic relationships is essential for personal and professional fulfillment. Authenticity involves being true to oneself and others, fostering trust and genuine connections. In a world where superficial interactions often prevail, cultivating authentic relationships requires intentionality and a commitment to vulnerability. By embracing authenticity, individuals can create meaningful and lasting connections that enrich their lives and contribute to their overall well-being.

One of the key components of authenticity is self-awareness. Understanding one's values, strengths, and limitations is essential for building genuine relationships. By being honest with themselves, individuals can present their true selves to others, fostering trust and respect. This self-awareness extends to recognizing and embracing imperfections, allowing for deeper and more meaningful connections. Authentic relationships are built on a foundation of honesty and vulnerability, where individuals feel safe to express their true selves without fear of judgment.

Empathy is another crucial aspect of building authentic relationships. By actively listening and understanding the perspectives of others, individuals can create a supportive and compassionate environment. This empathetic approach fosters mutual respect and understanding, allowing for deeper

CHAPTER 5: BUILDING AUTHENTIC RELATIONSHIPS

connections and more meaningful interactions. Authentic relationships thrive on empathy, where individuals feel heard, valued, and understood. By prioritizing empathy, individuals can create a network of support and connection that enhances their overall well-being.

Ultimately, building authentic relationships requires continuous effort and intentionality. It involves being present, listening actively, and expressing genuine interest in the lives of others. By embracing authenticity and empathy, individuals can create relationships that are both meaningful and fulfilling. These connections enrich their lives and contribute to their overall sense of purpose and belonging. Building authentic relationships is a virtuous venture that enhances personal well-being and fosters a sense of community and connection.

7

Chapter 6: Embracing Life's Challenges with Grace

Life is full of challenges and uncertainties, and how we navigate them significantly impacts our overall well-being and fulfillment. Embracing life's challenges with grace involves adopting a mindset of resilience and adaptability, viewing obstacles as opportunities for growth and learning. It involves cultivating a positive mindset, where challenges are seen as opportunities for personal and professional development. By embracing life's challenges with grace, individuals can navigate adversity with resilience and strength, ultimately emerging stronger and more capable.

One of the key components of embracing challenges with grace is resilience. Resilience involves the ability to bounce back from setbacks and adapt to changing circumstances. It requires a mindset of perseverance and determination, where individuals view obstacles as temporary and surmountable. By developing resilience, individuals can navigate life's challenges with confidence and poise, maintaining a sense of purpose and direction even in the face of adversity. This resilience allows for continuous growth and development, fostering a sense of empowerment and fulfillment.

Another important aspect of embracing challenges with grace is adaptability. Life is unpredictable, and the ability to adapt to new situations and environments is crucial for navigating uncertainty. Adaptability involves being open to change, willing to learn, and flexible in one's approach. By embracing change and remaining open to new possibilities, individuals can navigate challenges with creativity and resourcefulness. This adaptability allows for a more dynamic and fulfilling life, where individuals can thrive in diverse and ever-changing circumstances.

Ultimately, embracing life's challenges with grace requires a commitment to personal growth and development. It involves a willingness to learn from experiences, both positive and negative, and to continuously strive for improvement. By adopting a mindset of resilience and adaptability, individuals can navigate life's challenges with confidence and purpose, creating a life that is both fulfilling and impactful. Embracing challenges with grace is a virtuous venture that empowers individuals to lead a life of faith, ethics, and career fulfillment.

8

Chapter 7: Cultivating a Strong Work Ethic

A strong work ethic is essential for achieving success and fulfillment in both personal and professional endeavors. It involves a commitment to hard work, dedication, and integrity, ensuring that individuals consistently strive for excellence in their pursuits. Cultivating a strong work ethic requires a deep understanding of one's values and goals, as well as a willingness to put in the necessary effort to achieve them. By prioritizing hard work and dedication, individuals can build a foundation of success and fulfillment that extends beyond mere material achievements.

One of the key components of a strong work ethic is discipline. Discipline involves the ability to stay focused and committed to one's goals, even in the face of distractions or setbacks. It requires a mindset of perseverance and determination, where individuals consistently put in the effort required to achieve their objectives. By developing discipline, individuals can navigate the challenges of their pursuits with confidence and resilience, maintaining a sense of purpose and direction. This discipline fosters a sense of achievement and fulfillment, as individuals consistently strive for excellence in their endeavors.

Integrity is another crucial aspect of a strong work ethic. Integrity involves acting with honesty and transparency, ensuring that one's actions align with their values and principles. By prioritizing integrity in their work, individuals can build a reputation of trust and respect, fostering positive and supportive relationships. This integrity extends to all aspects of one's professional life, from interactions with colleagues and clients to the quality of their work. By maintaining a strong sense of integrity, individuals can navigate their careers with confidence and authenticity, creating a positive impact on their community and beyond.

Ultimately, cultivating a strong work ethic requires continuous effort and intentionality. It involves a commitment to personal growth and development, as well as a willingness to put in the necessary effort to achieve one's goals. By prioritizing discipline and integrity, individuals can build a foundation of success and fulfillment that extends beyond mere material achievements. This strong work ethic empowers individuals to lead virtuous ventures in both their personal and professional lives, creating a life of faith, ethics, and career fulfillment.

9

Chapter 8: Nurturing a Spirit of Gratitude

Gratitude is a powerful force that can transform our lives and enhance our overall well-being. Nurturing a spirit of gratitude involves recognizing and appreciating the positive aspects of our lives, no matter how small or seemingly insignificant. By cultivating gratitude, individuals can foster a sense of contentment and joy, enhancing their overall sense of fulfillment and happiness. This practice of gratitude extends to all aspects of life, from personal relationships to professional endeavors, creating a ripple effect of positivity and appreciation.

One of the key components of nurturing gratitude is mindfulness. Mindfulness involves being present and fully engaged in the moment, allowing individuals to recognize and appreciate the beauty and blessings in their lives. By practicing mindfulness, individuals can cultivate a deeper sense of gratitude for the simple pleasures and experiences that often go unnoticed. This mindfulness extends to all aspects of life, from the beauty of nature to the kindness of others, fostering a sense of appreciation and contentment. By prioritizing mindfulness, individuals can nurture a spirit of gratitude that enhances their overall well-being.

Another important aspect of nurturing gratitude is expressing appreciation. Expressing gratitude involves acknowledging and thanking others for their contributions and kindness. This practice of gratitude fosters a sense of connection and belonging, reinforcing the importance of positive relationships and mutual support. By expressing appreciation, individuals can create a positive and supportive environment, where everyone feels valued and respected. This practice of gratitude extends beyond words, involving acts of kindness and generosity that demonstrate appreciation and care.

Ultimately, nurturing a spirit of gratitude requires continuous effort and intentionality. It involves a commitment to recognizing and appreciating the positive aspects of life, no matter how small or seemingly insignificant. By prioritizing mindfulness and expressing appreciation, individuals can cultivate a sense of gratitude that enhances their overall well-being and fulfillment. This practice of gratitude empowers individuals to lead virtuous ventures, creating a life of faith, ethics, and career fulfillment.

10

Chapter 9: The Power of Compassion and Kindness

Compassion and kindness are powerful forces that can transform our lives and the lives of others. They involve recognizing and empathizing with the experiences and emotions of others, fostering a sense of connection and understanding. By practicing compassion and kindness, individuals can create a positive and supportive environment, enhancing their overall well-being and fulfillment. This practice extends to all aspects of life, from personal relationships to professional endeavors, creating a ripple effect of positivity and care.

One of the key components of compassion is empathy. Empathy involves understanding and sharing the feelings and experiences of others, fostering a sense of connection and mutual support. By practicing empathy, individuals can create a supportive and inclusive environment, where everyone feels valued and understood. This empathy extends to all aspects of life, from personal interactions to professional relationships, creating a positive and compassionate community. By prioritizing empathy, individuals can cultivate a sense of compassion that enhances their overall well-being and fulfillment.

Kindness is another crucial aspect of compassion. Kindness involves acting with care and consideration, ensuring that one's actions are guided by a desire to help and support others. By practicing kindness, individuals can create a positive and supportive environment, where everyone feels valued and respected. This kindness extends beyond words, involving acts of generosity and care that demonstrate a commitment to the well-being of others. By prioritizing kindness, individuals can foster a sense of compassion that enhances their overall sense of fulfillment and happiness.

Ultimately, the power of compassion and kindness lies in their ability to transform lives and communities. By practicing empathy and kindness, individuals can create a positive and supportive environment, enhancing their overall well-being and fulfillment. This practice of compassion extends to all aspects of life, from personal relationships to professional endeavors, creating a ripple effect of positivity and care. By embracing compassion and kindness, individuals can lead virtuous ventures, creating a life of faith, ethics, and career fulfillment.

11

Chapter 10: Leading with Integrity

Leadership with integrity is essential for creating a positive and impactful influence on others. It involves acting with honesty, transparency, and a commitment to ethical principles, ensuring that one's actions align with their values and beliefs. By leading with integrity, individuals can inspire trust and respect, fostering a positive and supportive environment. This leadership extends to all aspects of life, from personal relationships to professional endeavors, creating a ripple effect of positive influence and impact.

One of the key components of leadership with integrity is accountability. Accountability involves taking responsibility for one's actions and decisions, ensuring that they align with ethical principles and values. By being accountable, individuals can build a reputation of trust and respect, fostering positive and supportive relationships. This accountability extends to all aspects of leadership, from personal interactions to professional decisions, ensuring that actions are guided by a commitment to integrity and ethical conduct. By prioritizing accountability, individuals can create a positive and impactful influence on others.

Transparency is another crucial aspect of leadership with integrity. Transparency involves being open and honest about one's intentions and actions, ensuring that communication is clear and truthful. By practicing transparency, individuals can create a culture of honesty and trust, fostering a positive and supportive environment. This transparency extends to all aspects of leadership, from decision-making to interactions with colleagues and clients, creating a foundation of integrity and ethical conduct. By prioritizing transparency, individuals can lead with integrity, inspiring others to act with honesty and respect.

Ultimately, leading with integrity requires continuous effort and intentionality. It involves a commitment to ethical principles and values, as well as a willingness to act with honesty and transparency. By prioritizing accountability and transparency, individuals can create a positive and impactful influence on others, fostering a culture of trust and respect. This leadership with integrity empowers individuals to lead virtuous ventures, creating a life of faith, ethics, and career fulfillment.

12

Chapter 11: Pursuing Lifelong Learning

Lifelong learning is essential for personal and professional growth and fulfillment. It involves a commitment to continuous education and development, ensuring that individuals remain curious and open to new experiences and knowledge. By pursuing lifelong learning, individuals can navigate the complexities of life with confidence and adaptability, fostering a sense of empowerment and fulfillment. This commitment to learning extends to all aspects of life, from personal interests to professional pursuits, creating a dynamic and enriching existence.

One of the key components of lifelong learning is curiosity. Curiosity involves a desire to explore and understand the world, fostering a sense of wonder and discovery. By nurturing curiosity, individuals can remain engaged and motivated in their pursuits, continuously seeking new knowledge and experiences. This curiosity extends to all aspects of life, from personal interests to professional pursuits, fostering a dynamic and enriching existence. By remaining curious, individuals can continuously seek new knowledge and experiences, enhancing their overall well-being and fulfillment.

Adaptability is another crucial aspect of lifelong learning. Adaptability involves being open to change and willing to embrace new ideas and perspectives. By practicing adaptability, individuals can navigate the uncertainties and complexities of life with confidence and resilience. This adaptability extends to all aspects of life, from personal interests to professional endeavors, ensuring that individuals remain flexible and open to new opportunities. By prioritizing adaptability, individuals can cultivate a mindset of continuous growth and development, enhancing their overall sense of fulfillment and empowerment.

Ultimately, pursuing lifelong learning requires a commitment to continuous education and development. It involves a willingness to explore new areas of interest, seek out new experiences, and remain open to new ideas and perspectives. By prioritizing curiosity and adaptability, individuals can navigate the complexities of life with confidence and resilience, creating a dynamic and enriching existence. This commitment to lifelong learning empowers individuals to lead virtuous ventures, creating a life of faith, ethics, and career fulfillment.

13

Chapter 12: Leaving a Lasting Legacy

Leaving a lasting legacy involves creating a positive and impactful influence on the world that extends beyond one's lifetime. It involves a commitment to living a life of purpose and integrity, ensuring that one's actions and decisions contribute to the greater good. By prioritizing legacy-building, individuals can create a meaningful and lasting impact on their communities and beyond, fostering a sense of fulfillment and purpose.

One of the key components of leaving a lasting legacy is intentionality. Intentionality involves being deliberate and purposeful in one's actions and decisions, ensuring that they align with one's values and beliefs. By practicing intentionality, individuals can create a positive and impactful influence on the world, fostering a sense of fulfillment and purpose. This intentionality extends to all aspects of life, from personal relationships to professional endeavors, ensuring that one's legacy is rooted in integrity and ethical conduct. By prioritizing intentionality, individuals can create a lasting legacy that reflects their values and beliefs.

Service is another crucial aspect of leaving a lasting legacy. Service involves a commitment to helping and supporting others, ensuring that one's actions contribute to the greater good. By practicing service, individuals can create a positive and impactful influence on their communities and beyond, fostering a sense of fulfillment and purpose. This service extends to all aspects of life, from personal interactions to professional endeavors, creating a ripple effect

CHAPTER 12: LEAVING A LASTING LEGACY

of positivity and care. By prioritizing service, individuals can leave a lasting legacy that reflects their commitment to the well-being of others.

Ultimately, leaving a lasting legacy requires a commitment to living a life of purpose and integrity. It involves being intentional and deliberate in one's actions and decisions, ensuring that they align with one's values and beliefs. By prioritizing intentionality and service, individuals can create a positive and impactful influence on the world, fostering a sense of fulfillment and purpose. This commitment to legacy-building empowers individuals to lead virtuous ventures, creating a life of faith, ethics, and career fulfillment.

Virtuous Ventures: Building a Life of Faith, Ethics, and Career Fulfillment is a compelling guide for those seeking to harmonize their spiritual beliefs, moral values, and professional ambitions. This insightful book delves into the profound interplay between faith, ethics, and career, offering a roadmap for living a life of purpose and integrity.

Through twelve thoughtfully crafted chapters, readers will explore the foundations of faith and ethics, the journey of discovering one's life purpose, and the balance between spiritual and professional pursuits. The book emphasizes the importance of ethical decision-making, building authentic relationships, and embracing life's challenges with grace.

Virtuous Ventures also highlights the power of compassion, kindness, and gratitude in enriching our lives and the lives of others. It underscores the significance of leading with integrity, pursuing lifelong learning, and leaving a lasting legacy. Each chapter is filled with practical insights, real-life examples, and timeless wisdom to inspire readers to lead lives that are both fulfilling and impactful.

Whether you are at the beginning of your career, seeking a mid-life reinvention, or striving to align your professional life with your spiritual values, **Virtuous Ventures** provides the tools and strategies to navigate your journey with faith, ethics, and a sense of purpose. This book is a call to action for those who aspire to live virtuously, creating a positive and enduring impact on their communities and beyond.

www.ingramcontent.com/pod-product-compliance
Lightning Source LLC
LaVergne TN
LVHW020742090526
838202LV00057BA/6193